Song of Extinction

by EM Lewis

SAMUEL FRENCH

FOUNDED 1830

NEW YORK HOLLYWOOD LONDON TORONTO

SAMUELFRENCH.COM

ISBN 978-0-573-69738-8   Printed in U.S.A.   #29181

MUSIC USE NOTE

Licensees are solely responsible for obtaining formal written permission from copyright owners to use copyrighted music in the performance of this play and are strongly cautioned to do so. If no such permission is obtained by the licensee, then the licensee must use only original music that the licensee owns and controls. Licensees are solely responsible and liable for all music clearances and shall indemnify the copyright owners of the play and their licensing agent, Samuel French, Inc., against any costs, expenses, losses and liabilities arising from the use of music by licensees.

IMPORTANT BILLING AND CREDIT REQUIREMENTS

All producers of *SONG OF EXTINCTION must* give credit to the Author of the Play in all programs distributed in connection with performances of the Play, and in all instances in which the title of the Play appears for the purposes of advertising, publicizing or otherwise exploiting the Play and/or a production. The name of the Author *must* appear on a separate line on which no other name appears, immediately following the title and *must* appear in size of type not less than fifty percent of the size of the title type.

SONG OF EXTINCTION has been the recipient of the following awards and honors:

The world premiere of *SONG OF EXTINCTION* was produced by Moving Arts Theater Company at [Inside] the Ford in Los Angeles, California, from November 7 to December 14, 2008, with help from a Los Angeles County Arts Commission Winter Partnership Grant. The play was directed Heidi Helen Davis, produced by Kimberly Glann, (the co-producers were Steve Lozier and Cece Tio), with scenic design by Stephanie Kerley Schwartz, lighting design by Ian P Garrett, sound design by Jason Duplissea, oringal musical by Geoffrey Pope, and costume design by Laura Buckles. The stage manager was Jacqueline Moses The cast and production team were as follows:

KHIM PHAN	Darrell Kunitomi
MAX FORRESTAL	Will Faught
ELLERY FORRESTAL	Michael Shutt
LILY FORRESTAL	Lori Yeghiayan
DR. JOSHUA DORSEY	Tristan Wright
GILL MORRIS	Trey Nichols

(Note: With the playwright's permission, actors were cast to portray **KHIM PHAN'S** family in this production.)

Khim Phan's family:

SISTER	Aileen Cho
MOTHER	Sophea Pel
FATHER	Vance Lanoy
UNDERSTUDY	Brian Newkirk

Technical Director – Jim Bray
Master Electrician – Shannon Simonds
Publicity – Lucy Pollak
Graphic Design – Josh Worth
Still Photographer – Jay Lawton, JayPG Photography
Projection Design – Jessica Smith and Ian P Garrett
Sculpture – Kim Lyons
Solo Viola – Renata van der Vyver
Recording Sound Engineer – Barry Werger, Ullanta MusicWorks
Green Consultant – Jessica Aldridge

CHARACTERS

KHIM PHAN (55) – Max's biology teacher. Cambodian. He's been in the US since 1979.

MAX FORRESTAL (15) – Son of Ellery and Lily. Sophomore in high school. Plays the viola and piano, and has some talent as a composer. Wears glasses and appears uncomfortable in his clothes.

ELLERY FORRESTAL (47) – A biologist. Wears glasses and appears uncomfortable in his clothes.

LILY FORRESTAL (45) – Ellery's wife. Writes high school science textbooks. Has stomach cancer.

DR. JOSHUA DORSEY (28) – A doctor, just out of residency.

GILL MORRIS – CEO of a large corporation which owns (and plans to deforest) an area of the Bolivian jungle where Ellery Forrestal has worked for the last twelve years.

TIME

Present day

SETTING

Portland, Oregon
Multiple locations: office, hospital room, classroom, kitchen.
Golf course, bus stop, noodle shop, Bolivia

NOTES

The stage should be very empty and open, free of clutter. Spare, so each scene can slide straight into the next without pause.

Composer Geoffrey Pope has written a piece of music called "Disembarking" for the viola, to be used during the play. For permission and sheet music, Mr. Pope can be reached at www.geoffreypopemusic.com.

Page 85 of this acting edition contains alternate lines if a 'school-appropriate' version of the script is desired. Please note that these are the only places in the script that alterations of the text are permitted to occur. The remainder of the script must be performed as it has been written.

Scene One

(Darkness.)

(Then the slow, relentless rising sound of a metronome.)

(As the light rises, we see **KHIM PHAN***, a high school biology teacher, standing in an empty corner of the stage. With us, he is watching…)*

*(***MAX FORRESTAL***, a high school student, sits in the kitchen of the Forrestal house, holding his viola.)*

(Max's father, **ELLERY***, sits at the kitchen table amidst a raft of paper. He is unshaven and looks as if he's been up all night.)*

*(***MAX** *lifts his viola to his shoulder, and begins to play scales. For several measures, he stays with the beat of the metronome – but then begins to play faster. After a moment, he breaks off.)*

(Sets his bow hand on his knee. Looks over at **ELLERY***, but* **ELLERY** *doesn't look up.)*

*(***MAX** *begins again.)*

(He plays scales to the beat of the metronome for several measures, then begins to outpace it again. He stops. Takes a breath.)

*(***MAX** *begins again. Tries to play with the beat of the metronome, but can't. He plays faster and faster, cutting the bow violently against the strings. When he stops at last, he is breathing hard and his eyes are wild. He looks at* **ELLERY***, then turns away. Puts his hand to his head.)*

(The sound of the metronome continues.)

Scene Two

(continuous)

(KHIM PHAN *turns away from* **MAX,** *and looks out at the audience.)*

KHIM. There are things I know about extinction I don't know how to tell to my students. Maybe I'm afraid to tell. Hmph. Most chapters are easy for me to teach. DNA – easy. Cell structure – easy. This – I think too much. I tell myself, in my head, "It is not about you, dummy."

(beat)

Extinction is a very messy business. In books, it looks clean. First there is this animal. Then this animal goes away. But I remember extinction and it was not clean.

(beat)

It is not about you, dummy.

(beat)

You think science will be a safe place from memory.

(beat)

I am becoming an old man now. In teacher's lounge, the P.E. teacher, Mr. Henderson, gives me his chair if I come in and all the chairs are taken. I hate that.

(beat)

I have no children. No wife. No family. Maybe I don't want any. I just have these…These. These. I stand up in front of them in this classroom every day, seven thirty in the morning to three o'clock. Mostly biology comes out of my mouth. But sometimes I open my mouth and tell them…other things. How I stood, once, in a field beneath the Elephant Mountains, wide green field that smelled like grass under a wide blue sky and butterflies with yellow wings, glimmer glimmer in the sunlight came down and lit on me like I was a tree, like I was a butterfly tree, their soft feet settling on my skin like whispers.

(lights)

(KHIM *exits.)*

Scene Three

(continuous)

*(In the kitchen of the Forrestal home, **ELLERY** raises the remote control for his slide projector and pushes a button on it.)*

*(A slide of a nondescript endangered Bolivian insect is suddenly projected, very large, on the kitchen wall behind **MAX**. He looks up at the insect.)*

MAX. You need a better picture.

ELLERY. That's what it looks like.

MAX. Then you need a better insect.

*(**ELLERY** rubs his hands over his face.)*

*(**MAX** carefully places his viola into its case.)*

MAX. What time are you supposed to be there?

ELLERY. Ten.

(looks, suddenly, for his watch, and the wall clock)

What time is it?

MAX. Nine fifteen.

ELLERY. Why didn't you say something? I can't be late for this.

*(**ELLERY** leaps to his feet and begins stuffing the papers on the table into a leather knapsack.)*

MAX. You should shave.

*(**ELLERY** touches his hand to his chin, then disappears into the bathroom.)*

(Sound of an electric shaver come intermittently from off-stage.)

*(**MAX** exits the other direction, into the kitchen.)*

ELLERY. *(offstage)* What time does your bus come?

MAX. *(offstage)* Seven thirty.

*(**MAX** comes back out with a large, dusty can of sauerkraut and a can opener.)*

(He sets the can of food on the kitchen table, sits down, and stares at it.)

MAX. *(loudly)* This is the last actual food in this house.

(pause; to himself)

Tomorrow it will be ketchup.

*(**ELLERY** comes out, pulling on a fresh, but rumpled, white shirt. He buzzes his face some more with the razor.)*

ELLERY. Are you skipping school?

MAX. What do you care?

(beat)

I'm going to go see Mom.

*(**ELLERY** pauses for a moment, standing behind **MAX** and looking at him.)*

MAX. I'm going to go see Mom.

ELLERY. Get in the car. I'll drop you off at school on my way in.

*(**ELLERY** sets his razor on the kitchen table, and disappears into the bedroom, buttoning his shirt.)*

*(**MAX** opens the can of sauerkraut with the can opener, then takes some out with his fingers. After a moment, he puts it in his mouth.)*

*(**ELLERY** comes back in, wearing a suit jacket and holding a tie. He picks up his knapsack, and begins packing up the slide projector, then sees **MAX**.)*

ELLERY. What are you doing?

MAX. Eating breakfast.

ELLERY. Put that down! I have to go. I don't have time for this, Max!

MAX. Yeah.

ELLERY. Get in the car.

*(**MAX** stares at the table for a moment, then stands up. He grabs his backpack and his viola.)*

(ELLERY takes money out of his wallet. He holds it out to MAX, then, when MAX doesn't take it, he sets it on the kitchen table.)

ELLERY. That's for lunch. You can buy yourself lunch.

MAX. I hate everything about you.

(ELLERY closes his eyes for a moment, then exits toward the car.)

(After a moment, MAX takes the money and follows ELLERY out the door.)

(lights)

Scene Four

(**LILY FORRESTAL** *sits in her hospital bed, gazing out. Her hands are folded in her lap. She looks pale and fragile. Her head is wrapped in a scarf.*)

(**DR. JOSHUA DORSEY** *stands across the room from her, looking at her. He is wearing a white lab coat, and a stethoscope around his neck.*)

LILY. Stop looking at me.

JOSHUA. I'm sorry.

LILY. "Sorry."

JOSHUA. Do you…Would you like me to call someone?

(beat)

I could call someone for you.

LILY. Who would you call?

JOSHUA. Someone…

(beat)

You're married…

LILY. You are so dreadful at this that I'm beginning to think you've never done it before.

(**JOSHUA** *looks down at his feet.*)

LILY. *(laughs a little)* You've never done this before.

JOSHUA. No.

(beat)

We have a chaplain.

LILY. Shut up.

(**LILY** *looks away, looks at her hands, then looks across at* **JOSHUA.**)

JOSHUA. I'm fucking this up.

LILY. Yes, you are.

JOSHUA. I'm sorry.

LILY. You already said that.

JOSHUA. I had it written down, what to say, I talked with Dr. Keenan about it, but then I just...

(long beat)

Would you like me to send in the Chaplain for –

LILY. No.

JOSHUA. *(beat)* If you need anything, have them call. You can call. You can call any time.

*(**LILY** doesn't answer. She turns away.)*

*(**JOSHUA** pulls out his wallet and takes out a business card. He goes to the bed and carefully sets it on the blanket, then steps away from the bed.)*

JOSHUA. My cell phone number is on there. That's the one with my cell on it.

*(**LILY** nods.)*

*(After a moment, **LILY** feels along the blanket until she finds the card, and crumples it in her hand. She wipes her eyes with her wrists, but keeps her chin raised.)*

LILY. How long?

JOSHUA. It's hard to say, exactly...

LILY. Don't be a coward. How long?

JOSHUA. *(beat)* A week. Maybe less.

LILY. *(beat)* Ohhh.

(They are quiet for a moment.)

LILY. Go away now, will you?

*(**JOSHUA** nods, then turns and exits.)*

*(**LILY** wraps her hands around her middle and leans forward.)*

(lights)

Scene Five

(The slide of **ELLERY**'s *insect appears on the wall again.*
ELLERY *steps into its light.)*

*(***GILL MORRIS** *sits at his desk nearby, tipped back in
his chair.)*

ELLERY. I don't know how to explain this so you...

(beat)

Endemism is...Endemism is when a species doesn't
exist anywhere else. When it exists only in one place
in the entire world. Twelve years ago, I found a unique
subspecies of Dynastidae Strategus in the Bañados
del Izozog region of Bolivia. Discovered, not found.
Discovered. I was doing research there, trying to find
evidence of –

GILL. You have two more minutes, Mr. Forrestal.

ELLERY. I can't –

(beat; shoves his hand through his hair)

You can't cut it down.

GILL. Why not?

ELLERY. Look! Look.

*(***ELLERY** *pushes a button, and another slide appears
–* **ELLERY**, *grinning, standing by a battered tent in the
Bolivian wetlands, holding one of his insects in his hand.)*

GILL. Is that a slide projector?

ELLERY. This is twelve years ago. I've been monitoring the
species closely since then, I go back every year. For
three months every year, when they're hatching out
of their –

GILL. My grandparents had one.

ELLERY. What?

GILL. A slide projector. With one of those little fold-up
screens. They used to pull it out at family get-togethers
and make us watch slides from their cruises through
the Panama Canal.

ELLERY. They will die if you deforest the wetlands, Mr. Morris. They will all die. The entire species.

(GILL shakes his head.)

ELLERY. Wilson – from Harvard, E.O. Wilson – predicted that half of all species will be extinct in 50 years if current land use patterns continue.

GILL. It's a bug, Mr. Forrestal.

ELLERY. It's genocide.

GILL. You are being absurd!

ELLERY. You are killing an entire species.

GILL. The word "genocide" refers to people.

ELLERY. This is important!

GILL. It's a bug! It is a bug. If it was walking across my desk right now, I'd squish it with my *New York Times.* I don't care! You want to put two hundred and fifty Bolivian workers out of a job and let them starve to death because of a bug?

ELLERY. It's not about them.

GILL. No, it appears to be about you. The bugs…don't actually care.

ELLERY. The potential implications of the extinction of a species are –

GILL. *(overlapping)* You people piss me off.

ELLERY. *(overlapping)* – devastating. You can't know –

GILL. I can't know what?

ELLERY. You can't know what we might be losing if we were to lose an entire species. The cure for…The cure for cancer might be –

GILL. How many people live in Bolivia?

ELLERY. That has nothing to do with –

GILL. Nine million. Percentage of population living below the poverty line?

ELLERY. You're trying to –

GILL. Sixty-four percent. Percentage of arable land? Do you know what arable means?

(ELLERY turns off the slide machine and begins to pack up his things.)

GILL. Land fit to be cultivated; capable of producing crops. The percentage of land in Bolivia that is arable is 2.78%.

ELLERY. I don't know why you scheduled an appointment with me if you weren't going to –

GILL. Because I'm tired of you. *(waves arms)* The larger you. You people who have decided that because I am a responsible human being who owns his own business and makes a good living at it that I'm evil.

ELLERY. You are.

GILL. You're the one who wants to deprive two hundred and fifty Bolivian men from having a decent paying job, so they can support their families; the infusion of 7.9 million dollars into the Bolivian economy, not to mention what it will do for ours. Lumber. Houses. Cleared land that they can actually use to grow soybeans on, and rice, and corn. To eat.

(presses button on phone)

Gail? Mr. Forrestal is ready to go. Can you show him out for me? He's wasting my time.

(ELLERY looks at GILL for a moment, then picks up his projector and knapsack and exits.)

(lights)

Scene Six

(LILY is crossing her hospital room very slowly, leaning on a walker for support.)

(MAX enters. He stands at the door, watching LILY.)

(LILY turns her head a little, but MAX is just out of her range of vision. She talks over her shoulder.)

LILY. Max?

MAX. *(beat)* Yeah.

LILY. *(beat)* Don't watch me, or I'll get nervous and trip and fall on my ass. You don't want to see that, do you?

MAX. *(beat)* No.

(After a beat, MAX turns so his back is to LILY. LILY continues to move toward her bed.)

MAX. Dad is an asshole.

LILY. Max!

MAX. He's an asshole, and I hate him.

LILY. Take that back.

MAX. No. I'm not going to. And I'm not going home.

(LILY makes it to her bed and sits on the edge, breathing hard.)

MAX. He wouldn't let me see you.

(LILY stares at MAX for a long moment. MAX turns around and looks at her.)

MAX. I said, he wouldn't let me see you.

LILY. I heard you.

MAX. He had some meeting, and that was more important to him, and I told him that he's a jerk, and nothing he does means anything, and he dumped me off four blocks away from school, on Warrington and I had to walk, because he was late.

(LILY continues to look at MAX.)

(MAX shifts, then sets down his viola and backpack.)

MAX. Why are you looking at me like that?

LILY. What time is it?

MAX. Two thirty.

LILY. Are you cutting Biology?

MAX. It was…cancelled today.

LILY. *(harshly)* Don't you ever lie to me, Max.

MAX. *(beat)* Yeah.

LILY. Yes.

MAX. Yes. I'm cutting Biology. I know everything in that class already. I already know it.

LILY. Beside the point.

MAX. I wanted to see you.

LILY. Cutting classes is unforgiveable.

> *(beat)*

> Come here.

> *(**MAX** goes to **LILY**'s bed. He stands there, looking at her.)*

LILY. Do I get a hug?

MAX. I…don't want to hurt you.

LILY. You won't hurt me.

> *(**MAX** doesn't hug her.)*

MAX. You look…

> *(silence)*

> *(**LILY** looks down at her hands, then up at **MAX** again.)*

LILY. Mrs. Steinberg expects you at three fifteen.

> *(**MAX** nods.)*

LILY. I hope you've been practicing this week.

> *(beat)*

> Are you still working on the Chopin?

> *(**MAX** shakes his head.)*

LILY. Sit down and talk to me.

> *(**LILY** pats the bed beside her.)*

(After a moment, **MAX** *sits down in the chair by* **LILY**'s *bed.)*

LILY. Tell me what you're working on.

MAX. Dvořák. String Quartet #4 in E-minor.

LILY. What's he like? Dvořák. All the composers are men. Have you noticed that? I can name more women scientists then I can composers.

MAX. He...played the viola.

LILY. Like you.

MAX. Yeah. Yes.

LILY. What else?

MAX. *(pause)* He fell in love with one of his students. Then she got married to somebody else, so he married her sister.

LILY. Really?

MAX. You always like the parts that are like a soap opera.

LILY. Yes, I do. And I have no intention of apologizing for that.

*(**MAX** reaches out, suddenly, and takes **LILY**'s hand, without looking at her.)*

(a moment)

MAX. Your hands are cold.

*(**LILY** nods.)*

MAX. When are you coming home?

*(**LILY** looks at **MAX**, then away.)*

LILY. I...don't know.

MAX. I want you to come home. Or I'm going to – I'm going to run away.

LILY. No, you're not.

MAX. I hate him. I hate him. He doesn't care about –

LILY. Stop it!

MAX. – you. Or me, or anything, except his stupid bugs!

*(**LILY** presses her hand against **MAX**'s mouth, but he pulls her hand away.)*

MAX. I could take care of you.

LILY. No.

MAX. I could stay home and take care of you.

LILY. Max –

MAX. I can't stand it with him!

LILY. You have to go to school.

MAX. I don't have to.

LILY. Yes, you do! You are…

>   *(beat)*

>   You have to! You have to! You have to…

>   *(LILY starts to gasp, short of breath.)*

>   *(MAX pulls away from her, eyes wide.)*

MAX. I'm sorry!

>   *(LILY puts a hand up, but then uses it to pull her legs up onto the bed. She lies there for a moment, face turned toward the mattress. Breathing hard.)*

>   *(MAX looks at the door of the hospital room, then at LILY.)*

MAX. Mom?

LILY. Practice.

>   *(beat)*

>   You have…practice.

MAX. Yeah. Yes.

LILY. *(beat)* Come back tomorrow, Max. All right?

MAX. Dad won't drive me. I asked him today, and he wouldn't.

LILY. Because you had…school.

MAX. *(beat)* Yes.

LILY. Come after school.

MAX. Okay.

LILY. Okay.

>   *(MAX grabs his stuff, and goes.)*

>   *(LILY doesn't move.)*

>   *(lights)*

Scene Seven

(Sound of a metronome, unrelenting.)

*(**MAX** is practicing Dvořák with Mrs. Steinberg, but only he is visible, perched on a stool, viola tucked beneath his chin.)*

(Her voice is heard occasionally, but it is impossible to make out what she's saying. She's very far away from **MAX***'s thoughts.)*

*(After a moment, **MAX** puts his viola down on the floor. The music continues, along with Mrs. Steinberg's distant and occasional voice.)*

*(The lesson has not stopped, but now **MAX** pulls paper and pen out of his back pocket. He spreads the paper across the floor, and draws five lines across the first piece – a quick musical staff. He writes notes onto it, the music coming as fast as he can scribble. Composing.)*

(lights)

Scene Eight

(The sound of the metronome morphs into the sound of a heart monitor; softer, and less dependable.)

(It is night at the hospital. The lights are low.)

*(**LILY** is asleep in her hospital bed. **ELLERY** watches her from the hallway, through the window of her room.)*

*(**JOSHUA** walks past **ELLERY**, head down, scribbling notes on a chart. Then he pauses, turns, and looks at **ELLERY**.)*

JOSHUA. Mister…Forrestal?

*(**ELLERY** glances at **JOSHUA**, then back at his wife.)*

ELLERY. Yes.

JOSHUA. *(beat)* You can go in.

*(**ELLERY** shakes his head.)*

*(They stand there together for a moment. Watching **LILY** sleep.)*

ELLERY. I can see through her skin.

JOSHUA. That's because she's dying.

*(**ELLERY** looks at **JOSHUA**.)*

JOSHUA. You can go in. You should go in.

*(**ELLERY** shakes his head.)*

ELLERY. I had a meeting today. It didn't…

(beat)

She understands what I'm trying to do.

JOSHUA. Mr. Forrestal, your wife has cancer.

ELLERY. I know she has cancer. That's why she's here.

JOSHUA. We've done all we can.

ELLERY. *(beat)* No.

JOSHUA. I'm sorry.

*(**ELLERY** turns to go.)*

JOSHUA. Mr. Forrestal! Do you understand what I'm saying to you?

(**ELLERY** *glances back at* **JOSHUA** *for a moment, then exits.*)

(**JOSHUA** *watches him go.*)

(*lights*)

Scene Nine

(The next day. Biology class.)

*(**KHIM** stands at the front of the classroom, gesturing with a yard stick at a slide that shows a pictorial time line of species' evolution and extinction.)*

*(**KHIM** is speaking – lecturing – but we can hear only Bach's Concerto in D Minor for Two Violins and Orchestra – loud, powerful, overwhelming.)*

*(**MAX** sits at his desk. His viola is in its case beside him, along with his backpack, and he has the hood of his sweatshirt pulled up over his head.)*

(The bell rings – just audible over the music.)

*(**MAX** gets up, picks up his backpack and viola, and begins to exit.)*

*(**KHIM** takes two quick steps toward **MAX**, and extends his yard stick out in front of **MAX** to stop him.)*

*(**MAX** pauses.)*

*(**KHIM** pulls **MAX**'s hood down, then yanks the iPod earphones out of **MAX**'s ears. The music cuts out abruptly.)*

MAX. Ow!

KHIM. I gave a very nice lecture today, Mr. Forrestal.

MAX. I have to go.

KHIM. All about evolution of species.

(beat)

Chapter four in your book. Do you have your book with you today?

MAX. I forgot it at home.

KHIM. Forgot it at home today.

MAX. Yes! Mr. Phan, I have to go.

KHIM. I have to talk to you for a few minutes.

MAX. Maybe tomorrow we could –

KHIM. Sit!

*(**MAX** sits down at his desk, and looks at his hands.)*

(**KHIM** *leans against the wall, gazing down at* **MAX**.)

KHIM. Special projects in Biology are due next week.

(**MAX** *doesn't answer.*)

KHIM. I think maybe I should talk to you about this, because yesterday I don't see you. You go to English class, you go to Geometry, but Mrs. Brown didn't see you and I didn't see you. And today, maybe you were listening to something that was not biology on your headphones.

(**MAX** *looks at his hands, for a while, but then looks up at* **KHIM**, *who is gazing at him steadily.*)

MAX. What?

KHIM. What do you mean, what?

MAX. What are you doing?

KHIM. Trying to see inside your head.

(*pause*)

You are not doing well in this class, Mr. Forrestal.

MAX. I'm not stupid.

KHIM. I know. If you were this bad last year, you would be in Mrs. Rosenbaum's biology class for retards.

(*They are silent for a moment.*)

KHIM. What is that?

(**MAX** *looks up at* **KHIM**, *who gestures at his viola case.*)

KHIM. All the time, you carry that around.

MAX. It's a viola.

(*beat*)

It doesn't fit in my locker.

(*beat*)

I'll do the project.

KHIM. Twenty pages.

MAX. Twenty pages.

KHIM. I am here all the time if you need some assistance.

MAX. I don't.

KHIM. Twenty pages on the subject of extinction by 2pm next Tuesday, typed.

MAX. Yes! I have to go!

(**KHIM** *looks at* **MAX** *for a long moment, then gestures at him.*)

(**MAX** *grabs his stuff and goes.*)

(**KHIM** *watches him go, then taps his yard stick on the floor three times.*)

(lights)

Scene Ten

(Sunny, afternoon light.)

*(**GILL** is practicing his back swing on the golf course.)*

*(**ELLERY** appears, winded, and with his shirt torn.)*

*(**GILL** pulls back mid-swing.)*

ELLERY. Hi.

GILL. What in the world…?

ELLERY. Mr. Morris.

GILL. Mister…uh…Forrestal.

ELLERY. I needed to see you.

GILL. This is a private club.

ELLERY. I know.

GILL. This is completely inappropriate.

ELLERY. I know.

GILL. How did you know I would be here?

ELLERY. I misrepresented myself to your secretary on the telephone.

GILL. How did you get in?

ELLERY. I climbed over the fence.

GILL. You…

(beat)

What do you want?

ELLERY. You can't cut down my jungle.

GILL. It is not your jungle.

ELLERY. Yeah.

(beat)

Yes, it is.

GILL. It belongs to me. There could be some argument as to whether it belongs to the Bolivians. But the one person who has no claim whatsoever is you.

ELLERY. It's beautiful there.

(pause)

I forgot to tell you that. In my presentation. When we were talking before. Then your secretary said you couldn't meet with me again until February. Have you been there?

GILL. I –

ELLERY. It's beautiful there. The jungle is so thick you can't see ten feet in front of you, and the flowers are as big as your head.

(pause)

We took Max when he was seven years old, and again when he was eleven. I...Lily and I. We spent the whole summer in a tent that was pitched on top of a wooden frame so animals wouldn't wander in. Wild boars are bad on tents. They're a rooting animal.

GILL. Mr. Forrestal.

ELLERY. She would sit on the edge of the platform with her legs dangling over the side and write. She writes science text books. That's how we met. She was the only science major who was a girl. Max got brown as an almond. He wrote music in his head and hummed it to us at night while we listened to the dark.

GILL. It's already done.

ELLERY. What?

GILL. They did it today. The first swathe. They'll clear the rest of it by the end of the week.

(ELLERY puts his hand to his gut, like he's been punched.)

(GILL slides his golf club into his bag, then exits.)

(lights)

Scene Eleven

(**LILY** *is lying back in the bed, awake, but gazing vaguely out. She is now hooked up to an IV stand via a shunt in her hand and a heart monitor that beeps quietly.*)

(**JOSHUA** *sits in the chair beside her. He hands her some brochures.*)

JOSHUA. These are a few of the places in this area.

(**LILY** *looks at the brochures without opening them.*)

LILY. When?

JOSHUA. When will we transfer you?

LILY. Yes.

JOSHUA. We can do it any time.

> (*beat*)

Soon. Tomorrow, or the next day at the latest.

> (*beat*)

They're good places. They…know how to do this.

(**LILY** *gives* **JOSHUA** *a look.*)

JOSHUA. They can help.

LILY. What a terrible thing to be an expert in.

JOSHUA. *(beat)* Did you need someone to make the calls for you?

LILY. *(beat)* I won't see you again.

JOSHUA. They have their own doctor. We'll transfer all your records over.

LILY. I can't stay here?

JOSHUA. I thought you didn't like my bedside manner.

> (*beat*)

The insurance company requires us to…

> (*beat*)

I've delayed as long as I could.

(**LILY** *takes a deep breath.*)

JOSHUA. *(cont.)* There's home care…

LILY. No.

JOSHUA. You'd be able to stay in your own room. Your own place.

LILY. Until...

JOSHUA. Until.

LILY. No. They couldn't...

(beat)

They're still going to have to live there. It wouldn't work.

(beat; then hands him one of the brochures)

This one.

JOSHUA. This one?

LILY. Does it matter?

(MAX appears in the doorway, unseen by LILY and JOSHUA.)

(JOSHUA puts the brochure into his pocket.)

JOSHUA. *(pause)* You're my first one.

LILY. Your first what?

JOSHUA. My first patient. My first cancer patient. My first...

(beat)

I wanted to save you.

LILY. Romantic notion for an oncologist.

(JOSHUA looks at his feet.)

JOSHUA. I thought it would bode well. You know?

LILY. Maybe you should switch to accounting.

(JOSHUA smiles a little.)

JOSHUA. Late now.

LILY. Maybe you have to be a tilter at windmills to be in this profession.

JOSHUA. Maybe.

LILY. It's a rigged game, you know.

JOSHUA. Sometimes we force the windmills into submission.

MAX. Mom, what are you talking about?

(*LILY* and **JOSHUA** *both turn and see* **MAX** *in the doorway.*)

LILY. Max!

MAX. *(to* **JOSHUA***)* Where are you taking her?

(**JOSHUA** *stands up.*)

JOSHUA. Uh…hello, Max.

(**JOSHUA** *extends his hand to shake.*)

(**MAX** *smacks* **JOSHUA***'s hand away. He drops his backpack on the floor. He's in* **JOSHUA***'s face.*)

MAX. What are you talking about?

LILY. Max, it's all right.

MAX. I want to know when she's coming home.

LILY. Max.

MAX. Is she coming home now?

JOSHUA. I'm sorry.

(**MAX** *turns to* **LILY.***)*

LILY. *(beat)* I'm sorry.

(**MAX** *runs out of the room.*)

LILY. Max!!

(**LILY** *lunges out of the bed, after* **MAX.** *The IV pole crashes to the ground, the shunt pulls out of her hand, and she falls as she reaches the door, but struggles to stand again.*)

JOSHUA. Lily!

(**JOSHUA** *goes to* **LILY** *and puts pressure on her hand which is covered with blood.* **LILY** *struggles against* **JOSHUA.***)*

JOSHUA. Easy! Here – Let me –

LILY. Let me go!

JOSHUA. Stop! You're bleeding. We have to –

LILY. Max! I have to get to…

(beat)

I have to get to…

JOSHUA. Shh…

(LILY *tries for the door, and trails blood down it as she falls again.)*

(lights)

Scene Twelve

(KHIM stands in front of the board in his empty class-room. He still carries the yard stick, but leans on it now, as if it were a walking stick.)

KHIM. Today I talked about extinction. Logical conclusion to the chapter on evolution.
(beat)
During the whole life of this planet, between five and fifty billion species have existed. T. L. Erwin says there are maybe...forty million different species of animals and plants on earth right now. Normal extinction level, background level, is one species gone every four years. Right now? Thirty thousand species disappear every year. Become extinct. Thirty thousand species. Every year.
(beat)
This is why I assign a paper. I believe this is worthy of some thought. But they look at me like small animals. Deers. Pigeons. Wolves.
(beat)
When I came here, first thing, when I came here, to America, I met a man who was security guard for the court house. Uniform. Gun. Wisconsin. That's where I came to. Wisconsin. He told a story to me about going into the forest at night with a flashlight. He had a flash-light. Heavy. Black. On his belt. He said when he was a boy, he and other boys would go out into the forest at night and there would be possum. Small gray animal. Scurrying. And the boys would shine the flashlight in the eyes of the possums. And the possums would stop in the light. Very still. Not moving. And then the boys would hit them with a baseball bat.
(beat)
This is how I feel like I am sometimes when I stand in front of these small animals, these small student ani-mals, with large, terrible true things heavy in my hand like a stick.
(lights)

Scene Thirteen

(Night.)

(**LILY** *sits in her hospital bed, looking out the window.*)

(**ELLERY** *enters, walking fast. He stops abruptly when he sees* **LILY**.)

(They look at each other from across the room.)

LILY. Did you get my message?

ELLERY. Message? No...I...Is he here?

LILY. *(beat)* Max?

ELLERY. I know he's been –

LILY. Where's Max?

ELLERY. He didn't come home. So I thought...He isn't here?

LILY. No! I've been trying to call you for hours! Where were you?

(beat)

It's eleven o'clock at night! When did you see him? When is the last time you saw him?

ELLERY. This...morning. This morning.

LILY. This morning? You didn't notice until –

ELLERY. *(overlapping)* I had meetings all day. They didn't..

LILY. *(overlapping)* – now, you didn't notice he wasn't home? Why didn't you call me?

ELLERY. I thought he was in his room when I got home. I didn't know he –

LILY. Your meeting with Gill Morris is more important than your own –

ELLERY. You know what I'm trying to –

LILY. We can't let...

(beat)

Nothing can happen to him.

(**LILY** *puts her hand to her mouth, then down again.*)

LILY. He isn't answering his cell phone. I've been trying to –

ELLERY. He left it on his bed.

LILY. Did you call the police?

ELLERY. No. He –

> *(beat)*

> I thought he might be here.

LILY. He was here earlier. After school. He –

> *(beat)*

> Call the police, Ellery.

ELLERY. Maybe he's just at a friend's house.

LILY. He doesn't have any friends!

ELLERY. He could be –

LILY. Call the police!

> (**ELLERY** *picks up the phone, presses the button a few times to get a dial tone, then dials 911.*)

ELLERY. I'd like to report...

> *(beat)*

> Who is this?

LILY. Did you dial 911?

ELLERY. *(into phone)* I'm trying to call 911.

LILY. Who are you talking to?

ELLERY. *(to* **LILY***)* The hospital operator.

> *(into the phone)*

> I need to talk to the police, will you please transfer me?

LILY. *(beat)* What's she saying?

ELLERY. Shh.

LILY. Ellery?

ELLERY. I need to talk to the police. I don't understand why you can't just connect me.

LILY. What's she saying?

ELLERY. If the hospital was being taken hostage by terrorists, could you connect me?

(beat; unbelieving)

No?

*(**ELLERY** smashes down the phone.)*

LILY. What are you doing?

ELLERY. You can't make a call to the police from the hospital.

LILY. Cell phone. Where is your cell phone?

ELLERY. I never use it.

LILY. Do you have it in your bag?

ELLERY. I don't know.

*(**ELLERY** searches the compartments of his knapsack.)*

ELLERY. You're not supposed to use cell phones inside the hospital. It interferes with the –

LILY. I don't care!

ELLERY. Okay.

LILY. Maybe he tried to call you!

ELLERY. He knows I never use it.

LILY. Then what do we have it for?

*(**ELLERY** finds his cell phone and turns it on.)*

ELLERY. Here. Hold on.

(beat)

I'm sure he's all right.

LILY. You made him walk to the hospital. You wouldn't drive him.

*(**ELLERY** dials 911 on his cell phone. He paces as he talks.)*

ELLERY. Hello? *(beat; confused)* Highway patrol?

(beat)

No, I'm trying to...

(beat)

My...son didn't come home.

LILY. He's missing.

ELLERY. He's missing. I need to talk to the...

(beat)

Yes, the city...Yes.

(to **LILY***)*

He's transferring me.

LILY. Okay. Okay.

ELLERY. *(into the phone)* My son is missing.

(pause)

Five hours. Maybe six or seven hours. I don't know.

(pause)

Ellery Forrestal. His name is Max. Forrestal. Max Forrestal.

(beat)

F-O-R-R-E-S-T-A-L.

(pause)

If I knew where to look, I wouldn't have called you.

(pause)

They transferred me to you. I don't know why I got the highway patrol.

(beat)

Yes. It's a cell phone.

(beat)

No, I'm not in my car. It doesn't matter where...

(beat)

All right. I'm sorry. I just...I'm at the hospital. Saint Joe's.

(beat)

I'm calling from the hospital because...I'm calling from the hospital because my wife is in the hospital. Will you please just...

(Pause. Then **ELLERY** *puts his hand over the receiver and looks at* **LILY***.)*

ELLERY. They want to know his state of mind.

LILY. I don't know. He was...

ELLERY. *(into the phone)* We don't know. Will you just send someone, please, send someone, please?

(pause)

Room 517.

*(***ELLERY*** hangs up the phone.)*

ELLERY. They knew I was calling from a cell phone. It's funny that they can do that. I didn't realize they could –

LILY. Shut up.

(They are quiet for a moment.)

LILY. Did you call Mrs. Steinberg?

ELLERY. No. I don't know.

LILY. His viola teacher. Mrs. Steinberg.

ELLERY. I know who Mrs. Steinberg is!

(silence)

ELLERY. He wouldn't go there.

LILY. How do you know?

ELLERY. He doesn't like her.

(beat)

Maybe I should drive around. Maybe I'll see him if I drive around.

LILY. You can't...leave. The police are coming.

(beat)

I think it's my fault.

ELLERY. What?

LILY. I think it's my fault. He was frightened. Before. When he was here.

ELLERY. Frightened?

LILY. I wasn't – having a very good afternoon.

>*(beat)*

They want to move me to a hospice tomorrow.

>*(silence)*

>(**ELLERY** *moves toward the door.*)

ELLERY. Maybe I should drive around. Maybe I'll see him.

LILY. *(fiercely)* Don't you leave this room, Ellery Forrestal.

>(**ELLERY** *turns back toward* **LILY**.)

>*(a moment)*

>*(Then he sits down in the chair by the wall.)*

>*(lights)*

Scene Fourteen

(**GILL** *is back in his office. It's late. He has loosened his tie and poured himself a glass of whiskey.*)

(*A moment. Then he fits an earpiece to his ear and presses a button on his phone.*)

GILL. Gail?

(*A moment, then he smiles as she comes on the phone.*)

GILL. Still here?

(*pause*)

Me, too.

(*takes a drink*)

I wanted to…make sure you copied the Rosalvo files for the meeting tomorrow.

(*A moment. Then* **GILL** *takes his finger off the call button.*)

GILL. That's a lie.

(*presses button*)

GILL. (*to Gail*) That's a lie. That is a bald-faced lie, Gail.

(*pause*)

What I really want to know, is if we're going to have muffins at the meeting tomorrow.

(*beat*)

Muffins! Blueberry muffins! Keep up, girl.

(*takes a drink*)

No, I do not want bagels in addition to the muffins, nor do I want any other kind of muffins, but I do want coffee…

(*pause*)

No, I didn't call you just to talk about baked goods.

(*a moment*)

GILL. *(smiles a little)* Yes, I'm still here. Still here.

(pause)

Have you ever been to Bolivia?

(pause)

I don't know.

(drinks)

Get me a price, will you?

(beat)

On a ticket. A price on a ticket.

(beat)

I don't know. Wednesday.

*(**GILL** lets the button go. Drinks again, then exits.)*

(lights)

Scene Fifteen

(Sound of music in the distance, and voices, and laughter – a high school dance that's going on somewhere else in the building.)

(The lights come up on KHIM's classroom.)

(It is night. Late.)

(KHIM sits at his desk, grading papers.)

(MAX steps into the doorway, and stands there with his viola, watching KHIM. He's keyed up; his fist clenches against his leg.)

(KHIM starts when he notices MAX.)

(They don't say anything for a moment.)

KHIM. Max Forrestal.

(beat)

Are you here for the Sadie Hawkins Dance?

MAX. I need help with my project.

(KHIM glances at his watch.)

MAX. *(quickly)* It's okay. You don't have to. I can –

KHIM. No! Come in. Sit. I have a very boring life. No place else to be tonight. Don't tell Mrs. Coleman I'm here. She wanted me to be chaperone for the dance. Stand behind the punch table all night, and make sure no alcohol goes in.

(beat)

Sit down.

(MAX sits down at a desk.)

(They both realize at the same time that MAX has only his viola with him, not his backpack – no paper or pencil or books.)

(KHIM erases some old notes off the white board, then writes the word EXTINCTION in large red letters across it.)

(They both look at it for a moment.)

KHIM. So. Mr. Forrestal. Twenty page paper, due Tuesday, on the subject of extinction, yes? What is your thesis?

MAX. *(beat; very strongly)* Why do we even do this if we're just going to fucking die?

(KHIM turns and looks at MAX.)

KHIM. *(pause)* Good subject.

(beat)

Thesis should always be in the form of a statement, though.

(MAX laughs a little, but oddly.)

KHIM. Miss York…Did you have Miss York last year?

MAX. Mrs. Edwards.

KHIM. Mrs. Edwards. Very nice. Too much perfume. She talked to you last year in your English class about writing the essay. Yes?

MAX. Yeah. Yes.

KHIM. Thesis must always be in the form of a statement, which you prove or disprove, much like the hypothesis in science, which the scientist must prove or disprove. Greek word. "Hypo" is basis. "Thesis" is supposition. Basis for supposition.

(Beneath the word EXTINCTION, KHIM writes the words "hypo = basis" and "thesis = supposition.")

MAX. My Dad is a scientist. A biologist.

KHIM. I know.

MAX. You know my Dad?

KHIM. No. But on your last test, you wrote "I know all this already, my Dad is a fucking biologist."

(beat)

So. How do we take what you ask and turn it into a thesis statement?

MAX. I don't know. That's why I'm asking you.

KHIM. Don't act stupid.

MAX. Maybe I am stupid.

KHIM. I don't think so.

MAX. *(long beat)* There's no reason not to bomb the school and kill everybody because we're all just going to die anyway.

KHIM. "We're all going to die anyway" is one of your support paragraphs. Your thesis would be "I should bomb the school and kill everybody."

(beat)

Is this going to be your thesis for your paper on extinction, Mr. Forrestal?

(MAX looks down at his desk.)

(KHIM writes "I should bomb the school and kill everybody" on the board.)

KHIM. Maybe I should see if that is really a guitar in that case you carry.

MAX. Viola.

KHIM. Viola.

MAX. I was just joking. I don't need help with my paper.

(MAX goes to get up, but KHIM moves quickly around his desk and sits down at the desk beside MAX, putting one hand on his viola case.)

KHIM. Don't go yet.

(a moment)

KHIM. My father was also a scientist.

MAX. Don't try to be friends with me. You're not my friend.

KHIM. I'm your teacher.

MAX. Yeah.

KHIM. So you sit. I teach.

(MAX shrugs and glares, but slouches deeper into his chair.)

(KHIM goes around the desk and takes a pack of cigarettes out of his drawer. He opens the classroom window, and lights his cigarette, blowing the smoke outside.)

KHIM. Do you know where I come from?

MAX. Wisconsin.

KHIM. Wisconsin?

MAX. Last month you spent the whole period, one period, talking about cheese and the first time you milked a cow.

KHIM. That's a good story.

MAX. *(not agreeing)* Yeah.

KHIM. Everyone in Wisconsin is white. I am not from Wisconsin. I lived in Wisconsin for six years when I came here from Cambodia.

MAX. I've been to Bolivia.

KHIM. Nice for you, but not relevant to my conversation.

MAX. You're just talking. I don't care where you come from.

KHIM. All right. We'll go another way. There are many ways to skin a cat.

(beat)

Americans are very bad about understanding the concept of extinction.

*(**KHIM** draws in a deep lungful of smoke, then breathes it out through the window. He gazes out into the dark.)*

MAX. Okay. Why?

KHIM. Good question! Intellectual curiosity is good for the spirit.

(beat)

They do not believe it will ever happen to them.

MAX. *(beat)* What?

KHIM. You heard me. And you are not stupid.

MAX. We're not, like, dinosaurs.

KHIM. On the contrary, Mr. Forrestal. What makes you think we're any different?

(lights)

Scene Sixteen

(continuous)

(**KHIM** *carries his cigarette down into the light. He smokes.*)

KHIM. What to teach. How to teach. I do this thirty years and there is still a mystery to it.

(beat)

They will not ask questions. Students. High school students. If you teach high school, you must understand you will be teaching to purposefully blank faces for your whole life, and when they are not blank they will be angry. It's okay. That doesn't bother me. But like the rest of life, you will never know if you have done any good here.

(He takes a long drag on his cigarette.)

KHIM. I do not know if I do any good here. Fifty-five years old is a time for asking questions about this.

(beat)

My father was thirty-seven years old when he died, so maybe he never asked this question. My father the scientist. My mother was thirty-four years old. My brother was three years old. My sister was ten years old.

(beat)

But I do not teach ancient history. I teach biology.

(beat)

Teaching is a strange thing, though. You learn in school to teach one subject, you are hired to teach one subject, the class is called by the name of that subject – and you find, at some point, that you are teaching your self. Your whole self to them. My whole self to them, which includes biology, but also funny stories about milking cows with my host family in Wisconsin, who were very nice Baptist people. And bad, expensive addiction to cigarettes, which I hope they do not learn.

And Cambodia. Maybe I also teach them Cambodia.
Because...I don't know. Self-indulgence. Maybe. No.
I do not talk about it all the time. I do not talk about
it ever. But in this chapter on extinction, my country
and history and family come up bitterly in my throat.
And maybe I teach them about Cambodia without ever
saying its name.

(**KHIM** *stubs out the cigarette, and exits.*)

(*lights*)

Scene Seventeen

(Bolivia)

(Sound of birds and insects in the darkness – and then, also, a whacking sound, machetes against the underbrush.)

(The lights come up to reveal mist rising, and dense, green foliage.)

*(**LILY** – looking young and healthy – sits on the edge of the tent platform writing, dangling her legs down. She wears a tank top, shorts and boots, and her hair is down.)*

*(**ELLERY** walks slowly across to her.)*

ELLERY. Lily?

*(**LILY** looks up and smiles at **ELLERY**.)*

ELLERY. *(beat)* Where's Max?

LILY. *(gestures back toward the tent)* Sleeping. That hike wore him out.

ELLERY. I thought...I thought he was lost.

LILY. Never say that to a mother. How are the bugs this morning?

*(**ELLERY** turns and looks back toward the jungle – the sound of machetes is louder.)*

ELLERY. Extinct.

LILY. *(beat)* What are you talking about?

ELLERY. *(turning back to **LILY**; intensely)* I missed you.

LILY. You haven't been wearing your hat, have you?

ELLERY. No.

LILY. Courting sunstroke. Out here in the middle of nowhere. Miles from civilization.

ELLERY. You love it here.

LILY. Not if I have to drag you back to La Paz, 80 kilometers, on a travois, for medical attention.

*(**ELLERY** continues to gaze at **LILY**.)*

LILY. Come here.

(*ELLERY goes over to* **LILY,** *who puts her hand on his forehead.*)

ELLERY. I don't have sunstroke.

LILY. So you say.

(*ELLERY leans into* **LILY,** *and rests his head on her chest.*)

(**LILY** *runs her hand through his hair.*)

ELLERY. I think I'm dreaming.

LILY. You said that the first time we came here. Remember?

ELLERY. Yes.

LILY. Honeymoon in rubber boots and mosquito netting. Most girls wouldn't have gone for it.

(*The sound of the machetes gets louder.*)

ELLERY. (*pulls away from* **LILY**) Do you hear that?

LILY. Mosquitoes? I've gotten used to them.

ELLERY. Not the mosquitoes. Where's Max?

LILY. He's writing music in his head again.

(*Notes begin to sound themselves out on a viola, harsh and scraping, tentative at first, but trying to form into a piece of music. Trying to overwhelm the sound of the machetes.*)

LILY. He's just like you.

ELLERY. He's nothing like me. He never has been.

LILY. You have a miraculous ability to not see what's right in front of you.

ELLERY. He's like another country.

LILY. What is wrong with you?

ELLERY. I don't know…

LILY. You'd better hope he's not.

ELLERY. What?

LILY. You'd better hope he's not another country. I'm the one who always carries the maps and learns the foreign languages.

(**LILY** *doesn't seem to notice, but the music and the machetes get louder and louder.*)

(**ELLERY** *presses his hands to his ears.*)

LILY. Are you all right? Ellery?

(*The sound of the machetes against the undergrowth is very close and loud, now.*)

(**LILY** *leans down from the tent platform and shakes* **ELLERY**'s *shoulder.*)

LILY. Ellery?

(**ELLERY** *grabs* **LILY** *and kisses her fiercely. Desperately.*)

(**LILY** *is surprised, but doesn't resist.*)

ELLERY. Don't leave me!

LILY. Where would I go? Ellery, you're scaring me.

(*The trees at the far edge of the jungle begin to tremble and fall as the sound of the machete comes closer still.*)

(**ELLERY** *pulls away from* **LILY**, *and looks up in alarm.*)

LILY. Ellery! What's wrong?

ELLERY. Get in the tent!

LILY. What? I don't underst –

ELLERY. Get in the tent, Lily!

LILY. What's happening?

ELLERY. Now!!

(**LILY** *moves quickly back into the tent.*)

(*The underbrush shakes and falls.*)

(**ELLERY** *looks wildly toward the place where the chopping sound is coming from, then picks up a piece of firewood. He puts himself between the chopping sound and the tent.*)

(*lights*)

Scene Eighteen

(*Classroom*)

(**KHIM** *is at the window, smoking, like he was before.*)

(**MAX** *stands in front of the white board, gazing at the red letters written on it: "EXTINCTION," and "hypothesis = basis of supposition." Also his thesis statement: "I should bomb the school and kill everybody." After a moment, he rubs his hands across the board, smearing the words.*)

(*He looks down at his red hands.*)

KHIM. We have an eraser somewhere.

(**MAX** *wipes his hands off on his pants.*)

MAX. You're full of shit. People don't become extinct.

KHIM. No basis for that supposition. Better to say, people as a whole have not become extinct yet.

MAX. People are smart.

KHIM. You think so?

(*beat*)

You think that will help us?

MAX. We're not like some...stupid bug, who doesn't know enough to move somewhere else, and just sits there in the jungle, waiting to...

KHIM. Where would we go?

MAX. What do you mean, where would we go?

KHIM. If something happens here.

MAX. We have the whole planet!

KHIM. Not so big now. Nineteen fifty, we have less than three billion people here. Now, more than six billion. Two thousand fifty, projected more than nine billion. You see how this goes. This is many neighbors, each using resources, each taking up space, many, many people, and more coming. You think we're going to go live on the moon, now?

MAX. *(beat)* I don't know what you're saying. What are you saying? It doesn't make sense.

KHIM. Americans are no good at thinking about extinction.

MAX. What – you're some kind of expert now? Teaching at this stupid high school?

KHIM. Which you wish to bomb, according to your thesis statement.

(MAX looks at KHIM for a long moment.)

(KHIM puts out his cigarette, giving it careful attention, putting the butt in a little metal Altoids can and tucking it in his pocket.)

KHIM. I know something about extinction. Yes.

(After a moment, MAX goes over to his viola case, and kneels down on the floor beside it.)

KHIM. I do not know why you have a difficult year this year.

(beat)

Fifteen, yes? You are fifteen?

MAX. Yeah.

(MAX opens the viola case and stares down into it.)

(KHIM walks slowly over and looks over MAX's shoulder into the case. Nods. Props one hip on the edge of MAX's desk.)

KHIM. When I am fifteen, Khmer Rouge rise in Cambodia and take over the whole country. Communism. Red Cambodia. My countrymen take up guns and knives against our own people.

(beat)

You do not know this, maybe, because Mr. Kerr, who teaches history of the world, does not go past the Second World War. Too complicated after that. You do not know this because…why is it important outside country of Cambodia? Why is it important forty years later?

(beat; increasingly to himself, more than to MAX)

KHIM. *(cont.)* But this is my own lesson in extinction. In my country, which is not Wisconsin, one fifth of the population was killed by the red communists. Khmer Rouge. Maybe two million people. Estimations vary. Murdered, some, for being intellectuals, or members of government, or for no reason. Forced from their homes and cities. Made to work the land with no food.

(beat)

I remember my sister, ten years old, very sick, lying down on the cold, red earth, and we left her there, because they made us leave her there, even though I said I would carry her. Even though I tried to carry her. She reached out her hand, but she did not cry.

(beat)

Our dead were scattered across those fields. Their besach – spirits – follow us wherever we go, asking if we will feed them, asking if we will burn their bones so they may rest. But there is no rest.

MAX. *(long beat)* Shit happens.

(KHIM smacks MAX across the back of his head, hard.)

(MAX rocks forward, bracing himself with his hands.)

MAX. Just tell me what you want on the stupid fucking paper, tell me a subject and quit fucking with me, I can't think of any other subject, I can't fucking think, okay? Just tell me what you want me to write down.

KHIM. What is the matter?

MAX. *(laughs hopelessly)* I'm not writing about that.

KHIM. I am not asking you to write that, I am asking you to tell me.

MAX. You're supposed to be helping me with my paper.

KHIM. It is eleven o'clock at night, and here you are. And no one answers the telephone at your house all semester long. And you wear the same clothes for three days now. And you are skinny like you are starving, and nobody seems to notice, but I see. And I want to know.

(MAX pulls the twenty dollar bill that ELLERY gave him earlier from his pocket.)

MAX. I have food money right here.

(MAX stares at the twenty for a moment, then rips it apart.)

KHIM. Where are your parents, Max?

(MAX clenches his hands into fists, then smashes his fists into the floor. He grabs his viola out of the case and raises it up to smash it against the floor, but KHIM grabs him from behind, by the coat, and hauls him up and back.)

(a moment)

(MAX is breathing hard.)

(KHIM does not let go.)

(MAX pulls the viola close and holds it, and tries not to cry.)

(lights)

Scene Nineteen

(Hospital)

*(***ELLERY*** *is sleeping in the chair, with his coat over his shoulders.)*

*(***LILY*** *is awake, leaning forward in her bed with one arm around her middle, rocking slightly. More pale and fragile than before.)*

*(***JOSHUA*** *comes to the door. He glances at* ***ELLERY****, then at* ***LILY****.)*

JOSHUA. Hello.

*(***LILY*** *turns quickly toward the door, but then away again when she sees that it's not* ***MAX****.)*

JOSHUA. Are you all right?

(beat)

Mrs. Forrestal?

LILY. I thought you were done with me.

JOSHUA. The nurse said you were…having a rough night.

*(***LILY*** *leans back in the bed, very carefully, still holding her middle.)*

*(***JOSHUA*** *watches her.)*

JOSHUA. She said the police were here.

LILY. Yes.

JOSHUA. *(beat)* Is everything all right?

*(***LILY*** *looks up at* ***JOSHUA****.)*

LILY. *(beat)* Max is missing. He's…missing. My son, Max.

*(***LILY*** *suddenly curls in on herself, clutching at her belly.)*

*(***JOSHUA*** *goes over to the bed and checks the tube on* ***LILY****'s IV. He picks up the self-medicating button and clicks it three times.)*

*(***LILY*** *grabs it out of his hand.)*

LILY. What are you doing!?

JOSHUA. I was just –

LILY. *(overlapping)* Don't touch that.

JOSHUA. *(overlapping)* – giving you some pain medication. There's no reason for you to be –

LILY. I need to be clear right now! I need to think.

JOSHUA. You need to not have any stress on you right now. Stress is not your friend.

(beat)

Would you like me to...wake up your husband?

LILY. No.

JOSHUA. Is there...someone else you'd like me to –

LILY. There is no one else. Stop asking me that! Get out! Will you just get out?

JOSHUA. He isn't helping you.

LILY. People in glass houses shouldn't throw stones.

(pause)

He doesn't know how to do this.

JOSHUA. I didn't even know what he looked like.

LILY. He is...my husband. My husband. Have you ever been –

(beat)

No.

(beat)

If he fails at being my husband, it's nobody's business but ours.

(JOSHUA *goes to the door, but then turns back to* **LILY.)**

JOSHUA. I need to tell you...

LILY. *(long beat)* What?

JOSHUA. We made some of those phone calls for you today.

LILY. *(warily)* What phone calls?

JOSHUA. We contacted Linwood Hospice.

(beat)

The place you and I talked about this afternoon? They'll be coming in the morning to pick you up.

LILY. You did what?

JOSHUA. I called the –

LILY. What are you talking about?

JOSHUA. The place we talked about this afternoon, Mrs. Forrestal. The hospice.

(*LILY rubs her face, then touches her head to steady herself as she feels the morphine.*)

(*JOSHUA steps toward LILY.*)

JOSHUA. Would you like to lie down? I think the morphine is –

LILY. Don't come any closer!

(*beat*)

I'm not leaving until we find Max.

JOSHUA. Mrs. Forrestal, we –

LILY. (*overlapping*) He could come here.

JOSHUA. – need to move you to a place where –

LILY. This room is not going to be empty when he comes back here, do you understand?

JOSHUA. They're coming at eight. In the morning.

LILY. I'm not going!

(*LILY throws the plastic water pitcher from her night stand at JOSHUA.*)

(*ELLERY lunges up from his chair.*)

ELLERY. Lily!!

(*ELLERY looks at LILY, then at JOSHUA.*)

ELLERY. Max?

(*LILY's face crumples.*)

(*The two men look at her for a moment.*)

LILY. (*to JOSHUA*) I'm not going!

(*JOSHUA watches them for a moment, then exits.*)

LILY. (*quieter*) They can't make me.
(*beat*)
Can they?

*(**LILY** begins to cry. There is a long moment with just the sound of **LILY** crying.)*

*(**ELLERY** watches her impassively.)*

*(After a few moments, **LILY** wipes her eyes with her hand. Laughs a little.)*

LILY. Sorry.

*(**ELLERY** shakes his head.)*

LILY. My head feels so funny right now.

(beat)

I mean funny peculiar.

(longer beat)

Talk to me.

ELLERY. I…don't know what to say.

LILY. Say anything.

(a moment)

ELLERY. I was dreaming about Bolivia.

LILY. Just now?

ELLERY. Yes.

LILY. Bolivia…

(a moment)

ELLERY. Remember our tent? Up on the wooden platform?

LILY. Yes. *(beat)* It was like a little boat. I always thought of it as our little boat in the green sea of the jungle.

ELLERY. You'd sit up there and write.

LILY. Yes.

ELLERY. With your legs dangling over the side.

LILY. Pretending to write.

(beat)

Waiting for you to come back from watching the Dynastidae Strategus hatch from their tiny clutches of eggs… hatch from their tiny clutches…of eggs…

(**LILY** *clutches at her stomach again, and breathes shallowly.*)

LILY. This is not what we're supposed to be talking about. I feel so…peculiar. We…we have Max now. Where's Max?

ELLERY. The police are –

LILY. *(overlapping; looking at door)* The police?

ELLERY. *(overlapping)* – looking. They're looking.

LILY. It's a rushing feeling. Cold, humming, numbing, rushing… floating…I am…

ELLERY. *(long beat)* Lily?

(beat)

Do you want me to get the doctor?

LILY. No more doctors.

(beat)

He's decided to stop tilting at me…

(beat)

I am…unmoored.

(beat)

And mixing my metaphors. I have morphine in my metaphors, Ellery…Ellery…Ellery…

(**LILY** *reaches out her hands to* **ELLERY**. *When* **ELLERY** *doesn't come to her, she reaches farther toward him, very far.*)

(**ELLERY** *steps toward her and takes her hands.*)

(**LILY** *pulls* **ELLERY** *close and looks into his eyes.*)

LILY. *(long beat; in a loud whisper)* This bed is the boat now.

(beat)

Do you understand?

(**ELLERY** *looks at her warily.*)

(lights)

Scene Twenty

(In the darkness, the sound of rain, and something like Ayumi Hamasaki singing, through a tinny speaker, or maybe "Both Sides Now," by Dengue Fever.*)

(24-Hour Noodle Shop)

(The name of the shop is written in pink neon Japanese characters, along with the words "24-hour" in English. The light from the sign reflects on a large, rain-streaked window. It's still dark outside.)

(KHIM and MAX sit across from each other, with big bowls of soup in front of them.)

(MAX gazes at his bowl.)

(KHIM eats his soup. After a few bites, he glances up at MAX.)

MAX. We're just going to sit here and eat noodles?

KHIM. *(beat)* I'm hungry.

(KHIM eats.)

(After a moment, MAX picks up the odd little spoon. He tastes his first spoonful of soup tentatively, but then eats faster and faster.)

KHIM. Sh, sh, sh.

(MAX glances up at KHIM.)

KHIM. Easy.

(MAX watches KHIM eat for a moment.)

MAX. My mom has cancer and she's going to die.

(A beat. Then KHIM nods.)

KHIM. Where is she now?

MAX. Hospital. Saint Joseph's Hospital. Room 517.

KHIM. Mm.

MAX. *(long pause)* I don't know what to do.

KHIM. Finish your soup.

*See Music Use Note on Page Three

(**MAX** *looks down at his bowl.*)

(**KHIM** *looks out the rain-streaked window. As he gazes out, he sees himself in the window, from when he was fifteen years old, very thin and ragged, and still in Cambodia.*)

(**KHIM** *closes his eyes and turns away from the window. Then he absently pats his coat pocket and pulls out a cigarette. He puts it in his mouth.*)

MAX. Mr. Phan?

(**KHIM** *looks at* **MAX.**)

KHIM. Yes.

MAX. *(beat)* I don't think you're supposed to smoke that in here.

(**KHIM** *takes the cigarette out of his mouth and slips it back into the pack. He stands up.*)

KHIM. Come.

MAX. *(warily)* Where?

KHIM. I'm going to take you home.

MAX. No.

KHIM. Yes.

MAX. I'm not done with my soup.

KHIM. It's very late.

MAX. I'm not going back.

KHIM. What else will you do?

MAX. Not that.

KHIM. Tell me what else you can do.

MAX. I'm not going home.

KHIM. Then I'll drop you off at the hospital.

MAX. No!

(**MAX** *shoves away from the table and stands, hands grasping the wall under the window.*)

(**KHIM**'s *glance flickers up to his own reflection in the window, but then moves firmly back down to* **MAX.**)

KHIM. Countryman of mine, Haing Ngor, wrote a book about Cambodia. In his book he talked about a time when he was taken away by Khmer Rouge soldiers. Everyone began to cry, he says. Because they know what happens when people disappear. And at a certain point, there can be no more pretending.

(beat)

I think you are at the place of no more pretending now.

(**KHIM** *puts on his hat.*)

KHIM. Come.

MAX. No.

KHIM. You can't stay here.

MAX. *(beat; grinning darkly)* Maybe I can.

(points at sign)

It's a 24-hour noodle shop.

KHIM. Home or hospital?

(**MAX** *turns around and leans against the window.*)

MAX. *(beat)* I could stay with you.

KHIM. *(beat)* No, you cannot stay with me.

MAX. Why not?

KHIM. I'm your teacher.

MAX. So?

KHIM. I am not a babysitter.

MAX. I'm not a baby.

KHIM. Sound like one.

MAX. I could run away.

KHIM. Hmmph.

MAX. I'm not going back there with him!

KHIM. With your father?

MAX. I hate him.

KHIM. So you leave your mother? When she needs you?

MAX. You don't know anything.

> *(beat)*

She lied to me.

> *(beat)*

Just let me stay for a couple days. Okay? I'll be really quiet. I won't bother you. I'll sleep on the floor.

KHIM. *(sharply)* I said no. Not appropriate.

MAX. Appropriate? You smoke cigarettes in your classroom!

> **(KHIM** *takes another step toward the door.)*

KHIM. Home or hospital?

> **(MAX** *doesn't answer.)*

KHIM. These are all the places I am driving you, Mr. Forrestal. So now you come or don't come.

> *(A beat, then* **KHIM** *turns, and walks out the door of the noodle shop.)*

> **(MAX** *stands there, staring at the door. Then he looks around the empty shop.)*

> *(He picks up his viola case and holds it in his arms for a moment, but then sets it carefully against the wall.)*

> *(He leaves the noodle shop through the other door, not following* **KHIM***.)*

> *(The lights dim, leaving only the sound of rain, and darkness, and the reflection of young* **KHIM** *in the window.)*

Scene Twenty-One

(continuous)

(Darkness. Sound of rain.)

(The reflection of young **KHIM** *is joined by the reflections of his father and mother and brother and sister.)*

*(***KHIM*** *stands in a spotlight.)*

KHIM. So I leave him there.

(long beat)

What? You think I would take him home? Let him sleep in my spare room?

(beat)

I have no spare room.

*(***KHIM*** *takes the pack of cigarettes out of his pocket. Shakes one out, and lights up. Taking his time.)*

KHIM. Very nice Baptist family. Wisconsin. Did I say this story already?

(beat)

I am in Cambodia.

(long beat)

Then I am in a refugee camp in Thailand. Many people close together. I don't know. Classes in American language. I don't know.

(beat)

I lose some time, maybe.

(gestures with hand, time escaping, as he speaks)

Then I am in the air. Heart in throat. My first airplane. Flying through the dark. Then I am in Wisconsin.

(beat)

They are very…large people. Everything is…

(beat)

KHIM. *(cont.)* For special first meal, Mrs. Anderson makes Thanksgiving dinner, even though it is not Thanksgiving. Turkey and mashed potatoes. Gravy and stuffing. Cranberry sauce and green jello salad, soft bread rolls and candied sweet potatoes. The table is... *(gestures)* ... all food, beautiful with food, and large, smiling people.

(beat; takes a drag on the cigarette)

I am disappointment to myself most of anyone when I cannot eat.

*(**KHIM** tosses his cigarette on the ground and steps on it.)*

And then we are now.

*(**KHIM** takes the car keys out of his pocket and jangles them in his hand.)*

I drive through the rain. I park my car in the garage. I go in the door of the house.

(beat)

Twenty seven years I live there. And it is empty. I see now. Every room is...empty. I have nothing but spare room.

(beat)

So I go back again. Hurrying. Out the door, hurrying, out the garage, back through the rain to the noodle shop.

(lights)

Scene Twenty-Two

(continuous)

(Darkness. Sound of rain.)

(In the noodle shop, the reflections of young **KHIM** *and his family fade as the lights come up.)*

*(***KHIM*** *comes in the door and stops. He looks around – and sees the viola. But* **MAX** *is gone.)*

(After a moment, **KHIM** *crosses slowly to the table, picks up* **MAX***'s viola, then exits.)*

(lights)

Scene Twenty-Three

(sound of a heartbeat)

(Sound of a river, rushing like morphine through **LILY**'s *veins.)*

(Soft tones of EKG monitors morph into the sounds of chittering insects and bird song.)

(Hospital Room/Bolivia.)

(When the lights come up, **LILY**'s *hospital bed is a boat on the Bermejo River in Bolivia, passing through El Impenetrable, the impenetrable jungle. The bed is surrounded by green and verdant overgrowth.)*

*(***LILY*** kneels in the middle of the bed, clutching one wooden oar, and paddling occasionally. She looks forward, trying to see where she's going.)*

LILY. *(calling out)* Hello!

(beat)

Hello! Is anyone there? Max? Max!

(beat)

Ellery?

(beat)

Hello!

*(***GILL*** parts the branches and peers out of the jungle unexpectedly.)*

*(***LILY*** startles when she sees him.)*

LILY. Uh...Hola!

GILL. Hola!

LILY. ¿Cómo está?

GILL. Bien! Bien, y usted, señora?

LILY. Uh...Perdido? Lost?

GILL. English! Thank the Lord. Hello, hello!

*(***GILL*** steps out of the bushes and onto the river bank. He is wearing an expeditionary hat, and a drift of mosquito netting trails down over his shoulders.)*

(GILL grabs the tow line off the end of LILY's bed and holds it to keep her from floating farther downstream.)

LILY. I'm looking for Max. Have you seen him?

GILL. Max who?

LILY. My son.

GILL. Max Myson. Don't know him.

LILY. No, Max! My son, Max. Max Forrestal.

GILL. Afraid I can't help you there.

LILY. I don't understand where we are.

GILL. Bolivia?

LILY. Is that a question or an answer?

GILL. *(from Archibald MacLeish)*…how swift, how secretly The shadow of the night comes on…

LILY. What?

GILL. He's lost, too?

LILY. Max?

GILL. Yes! Max!

LILY. Yes. I think he…Yes.

GILL. Maybe he's just…*(gestures)* Going his own way. Forging his own path. Cutting his own –

LILY. He's just a boy. And he's lost. I don't want him to be lost.

(beat)

Lily.

GILL. Where?

LILY. No, that's my name. Lily. Forrestal.

GILL. Gill Morris. Nice to meet you.

(Silence for a moment.)

LILY. What brings you to Bolivia, Mr. Morris?

GILL. Trade. Deforestation.

(beat)

Someone told me it was beautiful here.

LILY. Do I know you? Your name sounds so familiar to me.

GILL. I get around.

(beat)

It's a long way from Concepción to Ascención, as they say!

LILY. What?

(GILL laughs.)

(LILY frowns.)

GILL. In 1912, President Theodore Roosevelt traveled on a river in South America called the Rio da Dúvida. The River of Doubt. Even though he never had any. On an expedition. We don't have expeditions anymore. Just trips. It's not the same.

(The boat begins to drift. LILY tries to hold it against the current with her paddle.)

LILY. The current is carrying me farther and farther away.

GILL. That's what rivers do.

LILY. I have to…find Max.

GILL. He's behind you now.

LILY. No! I can't go. I'm worried about Max. And Ellery.

GILL. Are you afraid?

LILY. Am I…I'm afraid for them.

GILL. And for yourself?

(LILY looks ahead, into the distance, where the river is taking her.)

LILY. Yes.

(A long moment. Then LILY reaches out her hand to GILL.)

LILY. Give me the rope. I think I…

(beat)

I think I have to go.

(GILL hands LILY the tow line.)

(The boat begins to move downstream again.)

(*LILY tucks the rope away and picks up her paddle.*)

(*GILL waves a little.*)

GILL. Vaya con Dios, señora. En su expedición.

(*After she's gone, GILL looks at the jungle around him. He reaches out and picks a large, bright flower, then holds it to his face. Breathes it in.*)

(*lights*)

Scene Twenty-Four

(Hospital room)

(LILY sleeps.)

(ELLERY sits on the edge of LILY's bed, holding her hand.)

(After a moment, KHIM appears in the doorway. His hat and coat are dripping with rain.)

(He carries MAX's viola.)

KHIM. Mr. Forrestal?

(ELLERY turns and sees KHIM, then stands abruptly. He stares at the viola.)

ELLERY. Where did you get that?

KHIM. My name is Khim Phan. I teach –

ELLERY. Biology.

KHIM. Yes.

(ELLERY moves toward KHIM.)

ELLERY. Where's Max?

KHIM. I…He's…

ELLERY. Is Max all right? Where did you get that?

KHIM. He came to the school.

ELLERY. Where is he?

KHIM. He hasn't come here?

ELLERY. No! He hasn't come here! You said he went to the school?

KHIM. Yes.

ELLERY. But…he's not with you?

KHIM. No.

ELLERY. Then where is he?

(beat)

We've been…looking for him. The police are…looking for him. He…

(ELLERY turns, looks at LILY, then leans on the bed-stead.)

KHIM. I hoped he would come here.

ELLERY. No.

(KHIM sinks down into the chair beside LILY's bed.)

ELLERY. He never leaves his viola anywhere. Sometimes he brings it into the bathroom with him.

KHIM. You called the police department already?

ELLERY. We called them. They're...

(ELLERY moves restlessly around the room.)

KHIM. *(strongly)* I didn't know if you would realize he was gone.

(ELLERY stops. Looks at KHIM.)

(a moment)

ELLERY. *(with sudden incisiveness)* Tell me exactly what happened.

KHIM. He came to the school. I told you.

ELLERY. What time?

KHIM. Two hours ago. Maybe two hours. Very late. But the dance was still going on in the auditorium, so not midnight yet. They stop at –

ELLERY. What happened?

KHIM. He...wanted me to help him with his paper.

ELLERY. In the middle of the night? What paper?

KHIM. Special project in biology, twenty page paper on topic of extinction. Due Tuesday. You don't know?

ELLERY. I've been...

(beat; glances at LILY)

What else?

KHIM. He was...not himself.

ELLERY. What do you mean, "not himself?"

KHIM. His mother is here. He is not himself.

ELLERY. He ran off?

KHIM. No.

(beat)

I took him for food. There is a noodle shop at Third and Everett.

ELLERY. You took him for – At twelve o'clock at night? Didn't you think we'd be looking for him?

KHIM. No, I did not! I did not think you would be looking for him, Mr. Forrestal. He is dressed in dirty clothes. He eats like he is starving.

*(**ELLERY** looks away.)*

(a moment)

ELLERY. Where is he now?

KHIM. I said I would drive him home or drive him to hospital. And he would not go either place. I…

ELLERY. You left him there?

KHIM. *(beat)* He is not there now. I went back and checked.

ELLERY. *(beat)* He's on foot. Right? He's on foot. Third and Everett. An hour ago?

KHIM. Less. Maybe half an hour. I drive…I drove here.

*(**ELLERY** goes to **LILY** and kisses her on the cheek.)*

ELLERY. *(to **LILY**)* I'll be back, all right?

*(**LILY** doesn't wake.)*

ELLERY. I'm sorry.

(beat)

I'll be back.

*(**ELLERY** pulls on his coat.)*

*(**KHIM** stands.)*

ELLERY. No. You stay here.

KHIM. What?

ELLERY. She didn't…want me to go. But I have to find Max.

KHIM. I…am not –

ELLERY. Somebody has to stay, and there's no one else.

(beat)

Stay with her. And don't let them take her anywhere! I'll be back.

*(***ELLERY*** exits.)*

*(***KHIM*** stares after him for a moment, then moves around the edges of the room uneasily. He glances at **LILY**, then at the equipment surrounding her. It sounds very loud, now, beeping and humming and whispering.)*

*(Finally, **KHIM** goes over to **LILY**. He stares down at her, then takes her hand. He holds her hand between his two hands gently, to warm it, then sits down on the edge of the bed beside her.)*

(lights)

Scene Twenty-Five

(Unbearable cacophony of music. Overwhelmingly loud. Discordant.)

(It is night. **MAX** *walks back and forth in the rain near a bus stop, which consists of one bench, and a dilapidated Greyhound bus sign with graffiti spray-painted across it.)*

(The music gets louder, and **MAX** *presses his hands to his head.)*

(He strips off his hooded sweatshirt, and throws it on the ground. Then he kicks off his shoes. He takes off his shirt, and then his t-shirt.)

(As he sheds his clothes, the music simplifies and clarifies until just a single long, sustaining note from a viola remains.)

(MAX *stands there in the rain for a moment, in only his jeans. Breathing.)*

(He sits down on the bench, then curls up on it, on his side.)

(When the sustained viola note reaches its farthest point, **MAX** *lifts one hand, and begins to compose the Song of Extinction in the air. The viola's voice follows his hand.)*

(music)

(Then the sound of a car, stopping, parking, overlays the music. Car door opening, then closing.)

(ELLERY *runs on, then stops ten feet away from* **MAX**.*)*

ELLERY. *(tentatively)* Max?

(MAX *stops moving his hand.)*

(The music stops.)

(MAX *looks over at* **ELLERY**.*)*

ELLERY. What are you doing?

MAX. *(beat)* Waiting for the bus.

ELLERY. Like that?

MAX. I don't need you!

   (beat)

   I don't need anything.

ELLERY. You need a bus ticket. Do you have a bus ticket?

MAX. I'll buy one on the bus.

ELLERY. They don't sell them on the bus. You have to have one already.

MAX. You don't know everything!

   (a moment)

ELLERY. Mom needs you.

   *(**MAX** closes his eyes. Curls farther in on himself.)*

ELLERY. Where do you think you're going? You are fourteen years old.

MAX. Anywhere but here. Where ever the bus takes me. You don't care! Stop pretending like you care.

ELLERY. You are…my son.

MAX. You don't even know how old I am! Fifteen! I'm fifteen years old. My birthday was last Thursday.

   *(**ELLERY** steps closer to **MAX**.)*

ELLERY. There isn't a lot of time, Max. I don't…I don't think there's a lot of time.

MAX. You haven't even looked at her in six months. Looked at her. You haven't even looked at her.

ELLERY. Your mother is –

MAX. Don't talk about her. You don't get to –

ELLERY. She's dying.

MAX. Shut up!

ELLERY. I had to leave her to come find you!

MAX. You left both of us already. You don't give a shit. You don't give a shit at all and I hate you.

   *(**ELLERY** rubs his mouth with his hand.)*

ELLERY. Sit up.

MAX. Fuck you.

(**ELLERY** *goes to* **MAX** *and pulls him up by his arm.*)

(**MAX** *glares at* **ELLERY**.)

ELLERY. Why aren't you wearing any clothes?

MAX. I couldn't hear with them on.

(**ELLERY** *looks at* **MAX** *warily for a moment, then turns away, and begins to collect his clothes.*)

(**MAX** *lifts his hand.*)

(*The viola's voice lifts.*)

(*When* **ELLERY** *turns back to* **MAX**, **MAX** *drops his hand, and the music is silent.* **ELLERY** *hands him his clothes.*)

ELLERY. Put them on.

(**MAX** *sinks down on the bench, holding his clothes in his arms.*)

(*We become aware, suddenly, of* **LILY**'s *bed [which is a boat] drifting near.* **LILY** *paddles closer. Watching.*)

(**KHIM** *sits behind her, as in a canoe.*)

KHIM. (*humming softly, then singing: "Everything around me is so dark, but I will see no shadow." from Lakmé, by Delibes.*) Qu'autour de moi tout sombre, Je ne veux pas une ombre.

(**ELLERY** *leans forward, suddenly, and takes the clothes from* **MAX**. *He sits down beside* **MAX** *on the bench, and begins to help him dress, one article of clothing at a time.*)

LILY. I remember when I was pregnant with Max. Large with Max. I never thought about that phrase "large with child" until I was large with child, and felt as sweet and heavy as a summer peach. I woke up one morning and Ellery was sitting in the bed beside me with one hand on me – us – and he said "Lil – this is the most important biology experiment I've ever undertaken."

(*beat*)

I started crying. Because I suddenly wasn't sure if he was going to be able to do this. And I was much too far along to turn back.

(When **MAX** *is dressed,* **ELLERY** *stands up. Looks around. Then exits.)*

KHIM. There are things I know about extinction I don't know how to tell to you. Maybe I'm afraid to tell.

(After a moment, **MAX** *looks over toward where his father disappeared.)*

MAX. Dad?

LILY. I don't know where we are, now.

KHIM. It's all right.

LILY. I can feel mortality beating its wings against my windows.

KHIM. Shh…

LILY. This is frightening. I'm frightened.

*(***ELLERY** *reappears, carrying the viola case.)*

*(***MAX** *grabs it from him. Clings to it. Looks at* **ELLERY.** *)*

ELLERY. I thought you'd want it.

*(***MAX** *nods.)*

*(***ELLERY** *and* **MAX** *exit.)*

*(***LILY** *and* **KHIM** *watch them go.)*

(The lights fade slowly on the bus stop, but remain bright on the boat.)

LILY. I don't know where we are.

(The two of them look around like the travellers they are.)

*(***LILY** *paddles a little. Pushing forward.)*

KHIM. Bolivia.

LILY. Bolivia?

(The boat drifts past the broken stumps of cut-down trees. Empty, deforested land.)

(The bank of the river becomes red. Like the ground is bleeding.)

*(***KHIM** *glances over his shoulder. There are white bones in the red earth.)*

KHIM. Maybe Cambodia.

(**LILY** *stops rowing.*)

LILY. You keep looking behind us.

(**KHIM** *looks forward.*)

KHIM. It gains on me when I do not pay attention.

LILY. What is it? *(beat)* You can tell me. I don't think anything can hurt me now. Everything is…

(**LILY** *reaches out her hand, but then pulls it back and shakes her head.*)

LILY. …farther.

KHIM. I…think you are on your journey now. I shouldn't…

LILY. Shouldn't what?

KHIM. Distract you.

LILY. Am I supposed to be rowing?

KHIM. The current will carry you.

(*beat*)

This is a terrible thing to be an expert in.

LILY. Boating?

(*pause*)

I'm glad you're here.

KHIM. Your husband asked me to stay.

LILY. Ellery?

(*looks behind her*)

Where is Ellery? Where's Max?

KHIM. Shh…

LILY. I don't know where we are!

KHIM. Place of no more pretending.

(*beat*)

Tell me what you see.

LILY. Flowers.

(*beat; smiles suddenly*)

Flowers. In the most unexpected places.

(beat, then with sudden clarity)

LILY. *(cont.)* This is as far as you can go.

(KHIM nods.)

(a moment)

(Then LILY lets go of the oars. She reaches back and takes KHIM's hands. She pulls them around herself. Lays back in his arms, until he's holding her.)

(a moment)

KHIM. Forty years, I hold no one in my arms.

(beat)

I do not know how I find myself here, in your boat, Mrs. Forrestal.

(a moment)

(Then butterflies with yellow wings begin to flutter and fall onto and around the bed.)

(The light narrows.)

(LILY smiles a little.)

LILY. Lucky, I guess.

(She closes her eyes.)

(lights)

Scene Twenty-Six

(Hospital room)

(The medical equipment is off now.)

(The jungle has receded, but yellow butterflies still litter the bed and floor.)

*(**KHIM** is still holding **LILY**.)*

(For a moment, he sits there, with her in his arms.)

*(**JOSHUA** appears at the door. He goes to the bed. Looks at **LILY**. Takes a deep breath. Then picks her up out of **KHIM**'s arms and carries her out of the room.)*

(silence)

*(**KHIM** walks over to where he's been speaking with us. Sits on the ground, rather abruptly. Takes out a cigarette. Plays with it.)*

KHIM. Theodore Roosevelt, twenty-sixth president, had a theory.

(beat)

Lamarckian model of biology, in the 1800's, said that it was new environmental conditions that allowed new species to evolve. President Roosevelt hypothesized that the harsh frontier conditions in the United States of America had created a new race of people. The American people.

*(**MAX** and **ELLERY** return to the hospital room. They stare at the empty bed for a moment. Then **ELLERY** grabs the back of **MAX**'s neck and pulls **MAX**'s head onto his shoulder.)*

KHIM. I tell this story about Theodore Roosevelt to Max Forrestal when he comes back to my class.

ELLERY. Shhh…

KHIM. We are not in this room now. But they live in this room. As I live in Cambodia my whole life when I do not see Cambodia for forty years. How do I say to him, "Do not live in Cambodia!!"

(MAX pulls away from ELLERY, wiping his face with his sleeve. He moves to a place between KHIM and ELLERY.)

(MAX is in two places at once, now, and two times: in the moment of returning to the hospital with his father, and in the classroom with KHIM a month later. There is something oddly still about him, and disconnected.)

MAX. I did the paper.

KHIM. Yes?

MAX. Yeah. *(beat)* Yes.

KHIM. *(beat)* Requirement for passing my Biology class.

> *(MAX takes a somewhat rumpled [but typed, 20-page] paper out of his back pocket. He hands it to KHIM.)*

> *(Khim looks down at the paper and reads.)*

MAX./KHIM. Extinction, by Max Forrestal.

> *(KHIM looks at MAX.)*

MAX. It's not very good.

> *(ELLERY stares at the empty bed.)*

ELLERY. You shouldn't leave me.

> *(beat)*

> I don't know what to do.

> *(KHIM reads.)*

MAX./KHIM. This is supposed to be a paper about extinction, but I'm writing about my father instead.

ELLERY. I don't know how to do this, Lily. Max is...

> *(beat)*

> ...and I'm...

> *(beat)*

> Oh.

KHIM. *(reading)* His name is Ellery Forrestal. He's a biologist.

MAX. Last month, he lost everything.

> *(MAX glances at ELLERY, then back at KHIM.)*

KHIM. *(reading)* Endemism is when a species doesn't exist anywhere else. When it exists only in one place in the entire world. Last month, the subspecies of Dynastidae Strategus that my Dad found in Bolivia, that didn't exist anywhere else, and that he'd been studying for twelve years, was totally wiped out by an evil land developer. And my Mom died.

(KHIM looks up at MAX.)

MAX. I lost some time, maybe, because...

(glancing at ELLERY)

I was at the...hospital.

(beat)

Then I was at the funeral. And my Aunt Velina was telling my Dad that she would take me, if he wanted. She would take me back to New Jersey with her and Uncle Phil and my cousins. If he wanted. And I thought...he would. I thought he probably would want that. Do that.

(Time shifts.)

MAX. Then we were in the car.

(ELLERY moves to the car. He is driving.)

(MAX watches him for a moment, then goes and sits in the passenger seat.)

MAX. You missed the turn.

ELLERY. I know.

(silence)

MAX. Where are you going?

ELLERY. To the grocery store.

MAX. Why?

ELLERY. To buy groceries.

MAX. Why?

ELLERY. Because we need groceries.

(pause)

I'm not letting you go with them, you know.

*(**MAX** doesn't answer. But he hears.)*

(Very slowly, through the following, the light goes down on the hospital bed, leaving only the yellow butterfly strewn stage and the three men.)

KHIM. The rest of the paper was written in a foreign language.

(beat; holds out pages)

Music.

*(**MAX** leans over, suddenly, grabs onto **ELLERY**'s jacket, and rests his head on **ELLERY**'s shoulder.)*

*(**ELLERY** takes a deep breath. He puts his hand over **MAX**'s hand, and keeps driving.)*

KHIM. He calls it the "Song of Extinction." Maybe this is not a song about becoming extinct, though. Maybe this is a song about becoming.

(pause)

I think maybe he will pass.

(The "Song of Extinction" begins to play.)

(lights)

End of Play

APPENDIX

SONG OF EXTINCTION
ALTERNATIVE TEXT

If a 'school-appropriate' version of the script is desired, alternative lines may be used in place of some of the more profane passages in the script. Please note that these are the only places in the script that alterations of the text are permitted to occur. The remainder of the script must be performed as it has been written. Replacements can be made as follows:

Pg. 12:

JOSHUA. I'm screwing this up.

Pg. 43:

MAX. *(beat; very strongly)* Why do we even *do* this if we're just going to *die?*

Pg. 43:

KHIM. No. But on your last test, you wrote "I know all this already, my Dad is...an effing biologist."

Pg. 53:

MAX. Just tell me what you want on the stupid paper, tell me a subject and quit screwing with me, I can't think of any other subject, I can't think, okay? Just tell me what you want me to write down.

Pg. 76:

ELLERY. Sit up.

    *(***MAX*** doesn't move.)*

    *(***ELLERY*** goes to **MAX** and pulls him up by his arm.)*

ABOUT THE AUTHOR

EM LEWIS won the 2009 Steinberg/ATCA New Play Award for her play *Song of Extinction* and the 2008 Francesca Primus Prize for an emerging woman theater artist for *Heads* from the American Theater Critics Association. She has been awarded a Hodder Fellowship at Princeton University for the 2010-2011 school year. *Song of Extinction* premiered at [Inside] the Ford in Los Angeles in November 2008, produced by Moving Arts; it was Critics Choice in the *LA Times*, won the Ted Schmitt Award for outstanding new play from the LA Drama Critics Circle, and was named Production of the Year by the LA Weekly Awards. It was also winner of the 2008 Ashland New Plays Festival and the 2009 EcoDrama Festival. In 2007, *LA Stage Magazine* selected Lewis as a Los Angeles theater artist to watch as two of her other full-length plays received their world premieres. *Heads* – a hostage drama set against the war in Iraq that Edward Albee called "provocative and wonderfully threatening"– received its world premiere at the Blank Theater; the *Los Angeles Times* named it one of the top ten productions of 2007. It has gone on to further productions in Chicago and Denver. *Infinite Black Suitcase* – which *Variety* called "…endearing and insightful" – received its world premiere at the Lillian Theater, produced by TheSpyAnts. Lewis is a member of Moving Arts Theatre Company, the Dramatists Guild, the International Centre for Women Playwrights and the Alliance of LA Playwrights. She lives in Santa Monica, California now – but she's from Oregon.

OTHER TITLES AVAILABLE FROM SAMUEL FRENCH

OOHRAH!
Bekah Brunstetter

Dramatic Comedy / 4m, 3f / Interior Set

Ron is back from his third and final tour in Iraq, and his wife Sara is excited to restart their life together in their new home. When a young marine visits the family, life is turned upside down. Sara's sister is swept off her feet; her daughter Lacey trades her dresses for combat boots, and Ron gets hungry for real military action. In this disarmingly funny and candid drama, Bekah Brunstetter raises challenging questions about what it means when the military is woven into the fabric of a family, and service is far more than just a job.

"The young scribe's talent and potential are obvious in this Southern-basted dramatic comedy about the war mystique as it plays out on the American home front…"
— *Variety*

"…Poignancy and terrific humor in both the writing and performances…"
— *TheatreMania.com*

"If there's anything that stands out about *Oohrah!* at the Atlantic Theater Company's Stage II, it's the off-Broadway introduction of playwright Bekah Brunstetter, whose play is a fascinating, original take on something we've come to see rather often nowadays: the war play…. Let's hope we hear her voice uptown again real soon."
— *NYTheatre.com*

"The play skillfully depicts how the demands of military service affect an individual family and society as a whole. Brunstetter's people are real and funny. She never condescends to them or treats them as symbols to put a point across…A big hurrah for *Oohrah!*
— *Back Stage*

"There have been plenty of plays about the Iraq War on New York stages in the past several years but few that deal as directly with the viewpoints of military families as *Oohrah!*... Bekah Brunstetter makes an impressively smart debut (no one could argue that she doesn't have dramatic chops)"
— *MusicOMH*

Breinigsville, PA USA
04 January 2011
252678BV00003B/18/P